Copy 2

Kralovansky, Susan Holt

The Book That Jake Borrowed

Due Date

DATE	ISSUED TO
SEP 3 0	Robbie H.
OCT 1 5	Trey Lawmaster M4
OCT 1 0	Craig W. M
NOV 2	Trey Lawmaster

Pelican Library

PELICAN PUBLISHING COMPANY

GRETNA 2018

First printing, August 2018
Second printing, December 2018

The word "Pelican" and the depiction of a pelican are trademarks of Pelican Publishing Company, Inc., and are registered in the U.S. Patent and Trademark Office.

Library of Congress Cataloging-in-Publication Data

Names: Kralovansky, Susan Holt, author.
Title: The book that Jake borrowed / by Susan Holt Kralovansky.
Description: Gretna : Pelican Publishing Company, 2018. |
Summary: Jake borrows a library book, drips jelly on it, and must
    face the consequences, as told in a rhythm reminiscent of The
    house that Jack built.
Identifiers: LCCN 2018005534| ISBN 9781455623259 (hardcover
: alk. paper) |
    ISBN 9781455623266 (ebook)
Subjects: | CYAC: Stories in rhyme. | Books—Fiction. | Animals—
    Fiction. | Behavior—Fiction. | Humorous stories.
Classification: LCC PZ8.3.K8613 Boo 2018 | DDC [E]—dc23 LC
record available at https://lccn.loc.gov/2018005534

Printed in Malaysia
Published by Pelican Publishing Company, Inc.
1000 Burmaster Street, Gretna, Louisiana 70053
www.pelicanpub.com

THIS

IS Jake →

THIS

IS the book

that Jake borrowed.

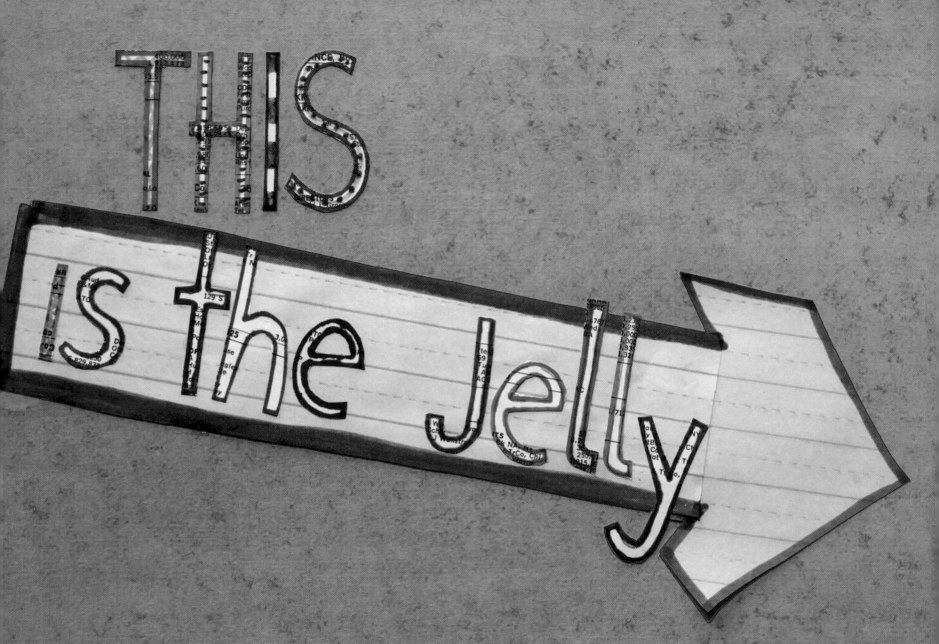

that dripped on the book
Oh, no!
that Jake borrowed.

that licked the jelly *Oh, gross!*
that dripped on the book *Oh, no!*
that Jake borrowed.

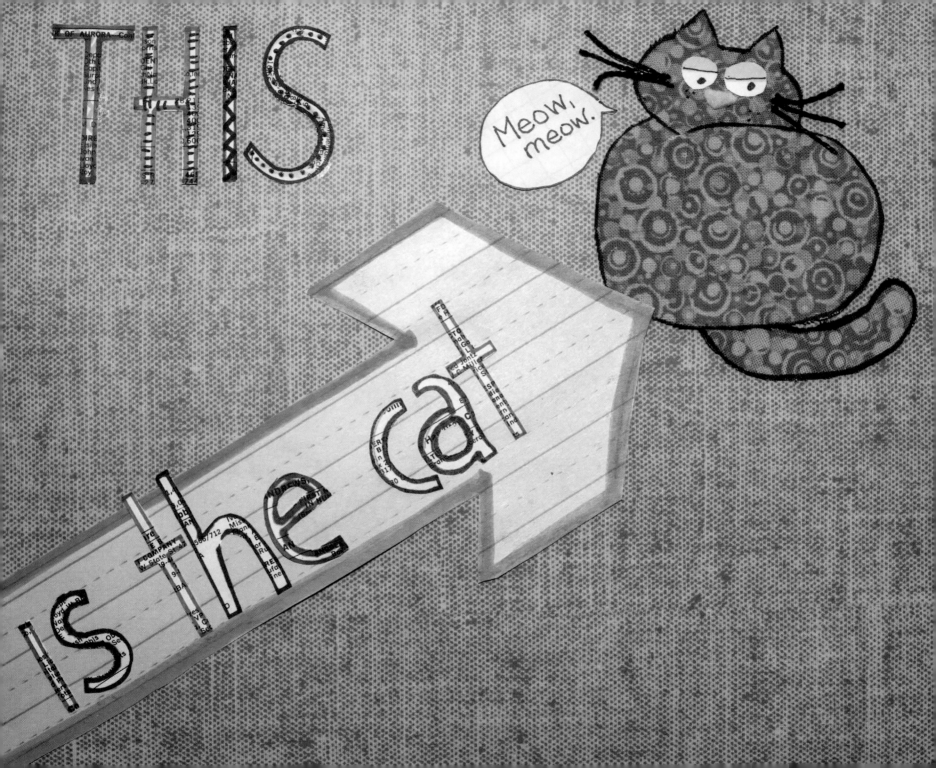

that caught the rat
that licked the jelly *Oh, gross!*
that dripped on the book *Oh, no!*
that Jake borrowed.

THIS

is the dog →

that chased the cat *Meow, meow!*
that caught the rat *Squeak, squeak!*
that licked the jelly *Oh, gross!*
that dripped on the book *Oh, no!*
that Jake borrowed.

THIS

IS the

book

Twelve Cowboys Ropin'
by Susan Hub Kochenbach

with the pages torn
that was chewed by the dog *Woof, woof!*
that chased the cat *Meow, meow!*
that caught the rat *Squeak, squeak!*
that licked the jelly *Oh, gross!*
that dripped on the book *Oh, no!*
that Jake borrowed.

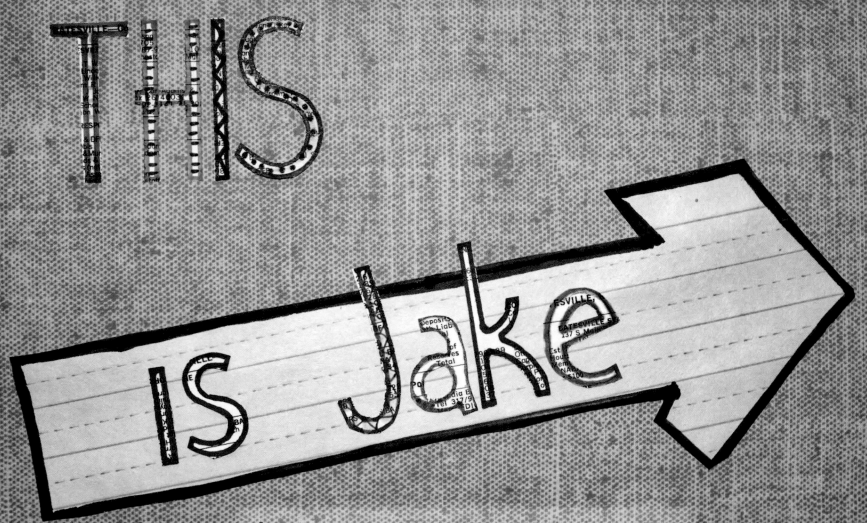

THIS IS Jake

the very next morn
holding the book with the pages torn

that was chewed by the dog *Woof, woof!*
that chased the cat *Meow, meow!*

that caught the rat *Squeak, squeak!*
that licked the jelly *Oh, gross!*
that dripped on the book *Oh, no!*
that Jake borrowed.

THIS
IS Jake's bank →

all cracked and worn
that pays for the book all tattered and torn

that was chewed by the dog *Woof, woof!*
that chased the cat *Meow, meow!*
that caught the rat *Squeak, squeak!*
that licked the jelly *Oh, gross!*
that dripped on the book *Oh, no!*
that Jake borrowed.

THIS → is the librarian

all forlorn
as she talks about books with the pages torn

with big jelly drips
that are licked by rats
that are chased by cats
and chewed by dogs—
those library books that kids borrow.

BUT, she's the

librarian

he adores.

She lets him have books,
not one but four

with no jelly drips *Oh, no!*
that are licked by rats *Oh, gross!*
that are chased by cats
or chewed by dogs—

wonderful books that Jake borrows.

book care rules

Don't eat or drink when reading a book.

Keep your books away from pets.

Keep your books in a safe place.

Use a bookmark.